ANNA,

TAKE NOTE ..

ORDERS.

LOTS OF LOVE AT
CHRISTMAS TIME

WRENN x

FOLLOW THE
PROMPTS, SCRATCH
OFF THE PANELS,
RECORD YOUR
THOUGHTS AND
DISCOVER 50 WAYS
TO SLOW DOWN

FOR BUSY BEES EVERYWHERE:
SLOW DOWN IN CASE YOU GET...

WHY ARE YOU SO BUSY?

SCRATCH OFF THE SEGMENTS THAT MOST REFLECT
YOUR ATTITUDE TO BEING BUSY

HOW MUCH PLEASURE DOES YOUR HECTIC LIFE BRING YOU?

WHY SO BUSY?

SCRATCH OFF THE
PERCENTAGE OF
TIME YOU DEVOTE
TO THE THESE THREE
PARTS OF LIFE

100%

0%

WORK

FAMILY

SOCIAL LIFE

ARE YOU HAPPY WITH THE BALANCE? HOW CAN YOU IMPROVE YOUR SCORE?

IS THERE ANYTHING YOU FEEL YOU HAVE MISSED OUT ON?

- _____
- _____
- _____
- _____
- _____
- _____

WHAT CAN YOU DO TO AVOID MISSING OUT IN THE FUTURE?

- _____
- _____
- _____
- _____
- _____
- _____

_____

_____

_____

_____

_____

_____

_____

_____

_____

_____

_____

_____

"THAT FEAR OF MISSING OUT ON THINGS MAKES YOU MISS OUT ON EVERYTHING"

ESTHER HILLESUM

_____

_____

_____

_____

_____

_____

_____

_____

_____

_____

_____

" THERE IS MORE TO LIFE THAN INCREASING ITS SPEED "

GHANDI

1. Notice the beauty in each day

2. More time to consider + think

3. Be less forgetful!

WHICH OF THESE WORDS MOTIVATE YOU?

PLEASURE

PRAISE

TRANQUILITY

LOVE

FUN

PERFECTIO

SUCCES

PEACE

Success

Praise

Perfection

Fun

"MY FAVOURITE
THINGS IN LIFE
DON'T COST
ANY MONEY.
IT'S REALLY
CLEAR THAT THE
MOST PRECIOUS
RESOURCE WE ALL
HAVE IS TIME "

STEVE JOBS

WRITE DOWN YOUR FAVOURITE THINGS IN LIFE

FIND 10 MINUTES EVERY MORNING TO SIMPLY SIT AND BE STILL

Set a timer, close your eyes, and take deep, regular breaths in through the nose and out through the mouth

AFTER TWO MINUTES DID YOU FEEL:

CALM?

ANXIOUS?

IF YOU CAN'T FIND
TEN MINUTES TO
SIT STILL, TRY TWO
MINUTES INSTEAD

DO NOT THINK
DO NOT PLAN
DO NOT WORRY

SIMPLY SIT
AND BE STILL

"ONE CANNOT THINK WELL, LOVE WELL, SLEEP WELL, IF ONE HAS NOT DINED WELL"

VIRGINIA WOOLF

SAVOUR EVERY

NEXT TIME YOU'RE EATING, TRY TO:

1. EAT AT A TABLE, PREFERABLY WITH A COMPANION
2. TURN OFF THE TV
3. CHEW SLOWLY AND MINDFULLY

_____

_____

_____

_____

_____

_____

_____

_____

_____

_____

_____

_____

HOW TO PUT THE BRAKES ON THE MORNING RUSH

- THINK ABOUT WHAT CAN BE PREPARED THE NIGHT BEFORE

- TRY GETTING UP 10 MINUTES EARLIER

- BUY SOME DRY SHAMPOO!

"IN THE NAME OF GOD, STOP A MOMENT, CEASE YOUR WORK, LOOK AROUND YOU"

LEO TOLSTOY

TAKE A WALK, YOUR DAILY COMMUTE PERHAPS

WRITE DOWN THREE THINGS YOU'VE SPOTTED FOR THE FIRST TIME

1.

2.

3.

ARE YOU WORKING EFFICIENTLY?

SCRATCH OFF THE
BARS FROM 0-100%
TO REFLECT WHAT
YOU SPEND TIME AT
WORK DOING

100%

0%

CHATTING TO
COLLEAGUES

EFFICIENTLY
FINISHING
TASKS

PANICKING

WHICH ONE THING WOULD HELP FREE UP TIME AT WORK?

HOW CAN THIS BE APPROACHED?

"BEING BUSY DOES NOT ALWAYS MEAN REAL WORK... SEEMING TO DO, IS NOT DOING"

THOMAS EDISON

IS BEING
████████████████████████

THE SAME AS BEING
████████████████████████

LEAVE

MOVE

FIND

SETTLE

BEFORE MEETINGS,
BEFORE PRESENTATIONS,
BEFORE OPENING YOUR INBOX
– ANY TIME WHEN YOUR HEART
MIGHT RACE:

1. SIT OR STAND STILL
2. LET YOUR BODY
    GO LIMP
3. LET YOUR GAZE SHIFT
    OUT OF FOCUS
4. COUNT DOWN FROM 20
5. REFOCUS

DISCOVER THE POWER OF:

_____

_____

_____

_____

_____

_____

_____

_____

_____

_____

_____

_____

_____

_____

_____

_____

" WORK EXPANDS TO FILL THE TIME AVAILABLE FOR ITS COMPLETION "

C.N. PARKINSON

FOCUS ON QUALITY RATHER THAN QUANTITY.
WHAT THREE TASKS OR ACTIVITIES WOULD GIVE YOU
THE BIGGEST IMPACT WITH THE SMALLEST INPUT?

1.

2.

3.

TRY TO ACCOMPLISH ONLY ONE THING A DAY.

THINK OF THE ONE MEANINGFUL THING YOU CAN ACHIEVE TODAY. WRITE OR DRAW IT HERE

LEARN TO SAY "NO"

MAY

	1	2	3	4	5	6
7	8	9	10	11	12	13
14	15	16	17	18	19	20
21	22	23	24	25	26	27
28	29	30	31			

AND PRE-BOOK DAYS IN YOUR DIARY
JUST FOR YOU

REMIND YOURSELF
OF WHO YOU...

WHO DO YOU TRULY CHERISH?

"YOU CANNOT BE
ALL THINGS TO ALL
PEOPLE. BE UNIQUE.
BE DIFFERENT. GIVE TO
OTHERS WHAT YOU WANT.
AND DO WHAT YOU WERE
MADE TO DO"

ROBERT KIYOSAKI

SCRATCH OFF A CHALLENGE AND RECONNECT WITH NATURE

SINK YOUR HANDS INTO SOIL

DO A LITTLE GARDENING

LIE DOWN ON GRASS

MORE

LESS

DO
MORE

" PEOPLE WHO WORK MUST TAKE THE TIME TO RELAX, TO BE WITH THEIR FAMILIES, TO ENJOY THEMSELVES, READ, LISTEN TO MUSIC, PLAY A SPORT "

POPE FRANCIS

PLEASURE IS NOT A
▬▬▬▬▬
IT IS A
▬▬▬▬▬

DRAW A PICTURE OF YOU DOING
EXACTLY WHAT YOU WANT

WRITE DOWN THE LAST FIVE TIMES YOU FELT JOY

1.

2.

3.

4.

5.

WHAT CAN YOU DO TO EXPERIENCE JOY MORE REGULARLY?

"WISELY AND SLOW, THEY STUMBLE THAT RUN FAST"

WILLIAM SHAKESPEARE

TAKE UP
SLOW HOBBIES

Stargaz

Origan

Garder

broide

Pott

WRITE DOWN THE BOOKS YOU'VE ALWAYS WANTED TO READ

LIFE IS
MORE THAN

THREE VERY LONG AND VERY GOOD BOOKS

REMEMBRANCE OF THINGS PAST
BY MARCEL PROUST

CLARISSA
BY SAMUEL RICHARDSON

LES MISÉRABLE'S
BY VICTOR HUGO

EMBRACE FREE TIME*

*DON'T IMMEDIATELY JUMP UP AND FIND ANOTHER SMALL JOB TO DO

NOTHING IS AS URGENT AS

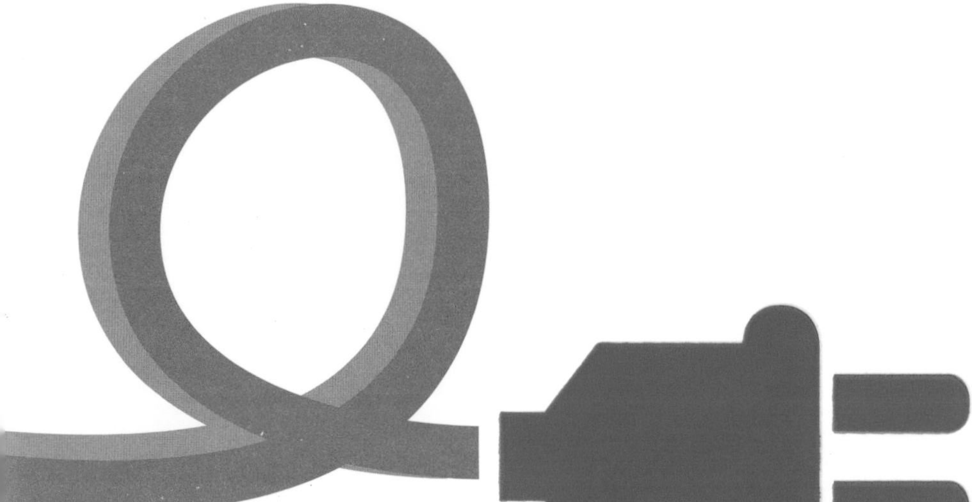

THREE STEPS TO A LIFE WELL LIVED

1. DO MORE THINGS THAT MAKE YOU FORGET TO LOOK AT YOUR PHONE
2. SPEND MORE TIME WITH YOUR FRIENDS AND FAMILY
3. REMEMBER TO STOP, REST AND BREATHE

SCRATCH OFF
A CHALLENGE

TAKE FIVE
DEEP BREATHS

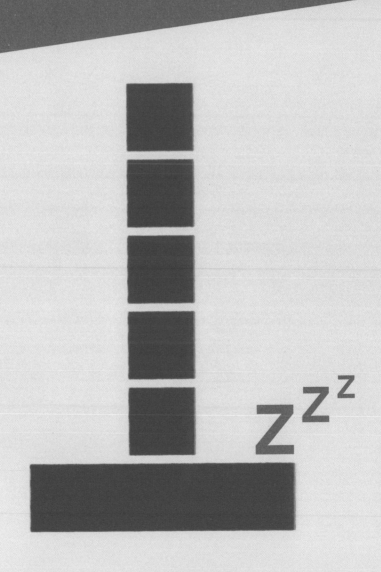

SEIZE
THE GIFT
OF A
RAINY DAY

WRITE A LIST OF JOBS THAT YOU'VE BEEN PUTTING OFF

WHEN IT'S SUNNY, TAKE THE TIME TO...

DRAW AN IDYLLIC LANDSCAPE –
THEN CLOSE YOUR EYES AND IMAGINE YOU'RE THERE

"THE FIRST PRINCIPLE OF ALL ACTION IS LEISURE"

ARISTOTLE

TIME IS
ON YOUR SIDE